HASTED'S HISTORY OF ORPINGTON

compiled by
John W. Brown

LOCAL HISTORY REPRINTS
316 Green Lane, Streatham, London SW16 3AS

Originally published in 1797 by
W. Bristow of Canterbury, Kent
as part of Volume II of
The History and Topographical Survey of the County of Kent
by
Edward Hasted

This edition published in 1997 by
Local History Reprints
316 Green Lane
Streatham
London SW16 3AS

ISBN 1 85699 142 3

INTRODUCTION

Edward Hasted was born on December 31st 1732, the son of Ann and Edward Hasted of Hawley, in Sutton-at-Hone, in east Kent. Edward's father was a wealthy barrister whose family riches had been established by his father, Joseph Hasted (1662-1732), who was Chief Painter to the Royal Navy at Chatham. It was through Joseph's skill in the financial markets that he amassed a large estate that yielded an income of £1,000 a year. The Hasted's came from an ancient Kentish family, branches of which are recorded in Canterbury's registers as far back as 1540.

Between 1740 and 1744 Edward was educated at the King's School in Rochester, after which he spent the following four years at Eton, completing his education with by two years at a private academy in Esher, Surrey. On leaving school in 1750 he briefly followed his father's profession as a lawyer and spent a short period as a member of Lincolns Inn in London.

Edward's father died unexpectedly at the age of 38 and the family subsequently moved to Rome House, near Chatham. In 1752 Edward returned to the old family home at Sutton-at-Hone where, in 1755, he married Anne Dorman, the daughter of a near neighbour. It was at this time that he began gathering the material from which he was to write "The History and Topographical Survey of the County of Kent", the first edition of which was published by Simmons & Kirkby of Canterbury, in four large folio volumes, between 1788 and 1799.

The publication was well received and before the fourth volume was issued Hasted begun work on correcting, revising, and extending the entries in the earlier volumes in order to produce a popular edition of his history in a more convenient octavo size. The smaller volume size meant that the books could be sold at a far cheaper cost than the large tomes of the first edition and hence they appealed to a much wider, general readership. It is from volume II of this second edition that this reprint of the entry for the parish of Orpington is taken.

The first three volumes of the second edition were published in 1797 by the Canterbury printer, W Bristow. Over the following four years another nine volumes were issued, with the twelfth and final volume being issued in 1801.

Such is the size of the work that Hasted spent the greater part of his adult life involved in gathering material and preparing the text for his history. His research began when he was still a young man in his twenties, and by the time the last volume of the second edition was published in 1801, he was an old man approaching 70. In between he had amassed a wealth of topographical material on the county from sources throughout Kent and London which filled more than 100 bound volumes.

No subsequent history of the County of Kent compares with the sheer size and breadth of content of Hasted's History. The twelve volumes of the second edition contain almost three million words, spread over 7,000 pages, containing an account of every parish in the county. This includes details of the prominent citizens of the area as well as a descent of the various manors and a history of the local church and clergy.

Hasted's achievement is all the greater when one considers the distressing personal circumstances surrounding his life between 1785 and 1807. During this period he left his wife of 30 years for the affections of Mary Jane Town. He was pursued by his creditors and subsequently imprisoned for debt. Following his release in 1802 he lived in poverty in a succession of cheap lodging houses until in 1807, his old fiend and patron, the Earl of Radnor, presented him with the Mastership of Lady Hungerford's Hospital at Corsham in Wiltshire.

Edward died at the Master's lodge at Corsham on 14th January 1812 aged 79. His son, the Rev. Edward Hasted, was present at his death and buried his father in the local parish graveyard. In 1929 a monument was erected at Corsham in Hasted's memory by Dr. F. W. Cock of Appledore with the support of the Kent Archaeological Society.

Hasted was a loyal son of Kent and considered his home county to stand "foremost in the rank of all others, so deservedly proud of its pre-eminence in every respect." His History is a fitting testimonial of his love for his county and the fact that no work of similar size and stature has been published since emphasises the magnitude of his achievement.

JOHN W BROWN

THE HISTORY

AND TOPOGRAPHICAL SURVEY

OF THE

COUNTY OF KENT.

CONTAINING THE
ANTIENT AND PRESENT STATE OF IT,
CIVIL AND ECCLESIASTICAL;
COLLECTED FROM PUBLIC RECORDS,
AND OTHER AUTHORITIES:
ILLUSTRATED WITH MAPS, VIEWS, ANTIQUITIES, &c.

ORPINGTON

ADJOINING to Chelsfield, northward, lies Orpington. The name of this place is corrupted from its original, which was Dorpentune, a name partly British and partly Saxon, signifying, the village, or street, where the head or spring of water rises. In Domesday it is called Orpintun, and in old deeds and charters, Orpyntone, and Orpedingtune.

This parish is very extensive. The village, which is of some length, and very populous, lies in the valley, having the church, Mr. Carew's house on the east side of it; near which, northward, is the house of *Barkhart*. On the hills, at the eastern extremity of the parish, is East-hall; and at the western, among the woods, the manor of Crofton. At Newell, a little to the westward of the village, the river Cray, so called from the Saxon word *Crecca*, signifying a small brook or rivulet, takes its rise, and running from thence almost due north, it passes through the several parishes of Cray, (to which it gives name) to Bexley and Crayford, where it crosses the London road, and then joining the river Darent below the town of Dartford, it flows in one channel with that stream into the Thames, nearly opposite to Purfleet in Essex.

A small part of this parish is in the liberty of the duchy of Lancaster, and the rest of it in that of the archbishop of Canterbury, which claims over the manor of Orpington.

The *manor of Orpington*, otherwise called Orpington Magna, or Great Orpington, extends likewise over the parishes of Hayes, Downe, Nockholt, and St. Mary Cray, which are accounted appendages to it.

In the year 1032 Eadsy, a priest, with the consent of king Canute, and Ælfgife his queen, gave his land at Orpedingtune, which he bought with eighty marcs of white silver, by *hustings* weight, for the good of his soul, to the monastery of Christ Church in Canterbury, to God's servants, for garment land.[m]

Odo, bishop of Baieux, the king's half-brother, and earl of Kent, among other acts of tyranny and oppression which he committed, through the greatness of his power, seized on several manors and possessions belonging to the churches of Canterbury and Rochester, and added them to his own domains.[n] From the former he took this manor of Orpington, which, however, he was not suffered to keep long; for on the promotion of Lanfranc to the see of Canterbury, in the room of archbishop Stigand, he forced Odo to restore to both those churches whatever he had robbed them of, in a solemn judicial assembly of the whole county, convened by the king's special command for this purpose, in the year 1076, at Pinenden-heath; at which the liberties of the archbishop, and his church, were solemnly confirmed to both of them.

Archbishop Lanfranc, among other regulations which he made for the future good government of this mo-

[m] Hustingi pondus, standard weight. See this grant, in Somner's Roman Ports, p. 72, and his Gavelkind, p. 215.
[n] Reg. Roff. p. 27.

nastery,

naftery, made a division of the manors and poffeffions of his church; for before this, the archbifhop and his monks lived together as one family, and had their revenues in common; one part of which he allotted for the maintenance of himfelf and his fucceffors in the archbifhopric, and the other to the monks for their fubfiftence, cloathing, and other neceffary ufes of their monaftery, in the proportion they now ftand recorded in Domefday, under the general titles of each.

In Somner's Gavelkind is a petition from the fubprior and monks of Chrift Church, Canterbury, to king Henry II. on occafion of the difpute between them and archbifhop Baldwin; wherein they affert, that archbifhop Theodore (who was elected in 668) firft parted the lands belonging to the church between himfelf and the monaftery, affigning to each their refpective fhare; and that the reafon of archbifhop Lanfranc's having been faid to have made this divifion was, that when the Normans, having conquered England, had feized on all the lands of the church, king William refigned them, at the inftance of Lanfranc, who reftored to each church what before they had poffeffed; but retained to himfelf what had been poffeffed by his predeceffors.

In this partition this manor fell to the fhare of the monks; and it is accordingly entered, under the title of the land of the monks of the archbifhop, as follows, in Domefday-Book:

The archbifhop of Canterbury holds Orpintun. It was taxed at three fulings in the time of king Edward the Confeffor, and now at two fulings and a half. The arable land is.... In demefne there are 2 carucates, and 46 villeins, with 25 borderers, having 23 carucates. There are 3 mills of 16 fhillings and 4 pence, and 10 acres of meadow, and 5 dens of wood, fufficient for the pannage of 50 hogs. In the whole value in the time of king Edward the Confeffor it was worth 15 pounds, when he received it 8 pounds, and now 25 pounds, and yet it pays 28 pounds. There are two churches.

King

King John, by his letters patent, dated at Romney, in his 7th year, granted to the prior and monks a market weekly, on a Wednesday, at this manor.

King Edward II. in his 10th year, granted and confirmed to them, and their successors, for ever, *free-warren* in such of their demesne lands as they were possessed of in Orpinton in the time of his grandfather.[p]

William Selling, who was elected prior of Christ Church in 1471, made great improvements at the several manors belonging to his church, especially at the apartments of the prior in this manor. In which state it continued till the final dissolution of this great monastery, in the 31st year of king Henry VIII. when it was surrendered into the hands of the king's commissioners, by Thomas Goldwell, then prior, and the convent; together with the manors, lands, and revenues belonging to it. All which were confirmed to the king and his heirs, by the general words of the act passed the same year, specially for that purpose.

The manor of Orpington being thus vested in the crown, stayed there but a short time; for it was granted, with its appendages, in the parishes and hamlets of Orpington, Okeholt, St. Mary Cray, Lynkill, Downe, and Heze, among other premises, by that prince, in his 32d year, to Percival Hart, of Lullingstone, esq. at the yearly rent of one hundred shillings, one penny, and three farthings, to hold *in capite*.[q] From him it descended lineally to Percival Hart, of Lullingstone, esq. who leaving an only daughter and heir, she carried this manor, with its appendages, in marriage to her second husband, Sir Thomas Dyke, bart. of Horeham, in Sussex, whose only surviving son, Sir John Dixon Dyke, bart. of Lullingstone, is the present possessor of it.

[o] Rot. Cart. ejus an. memb. 2, No. 14. Regist. Eccles. Christi, Cart. 131.   [p] Ibid. Regist. Cart. 134.
[q] Rot. Esch. ejus anni, pt. 5.

Sir Percival Hart, knight of the body to king Henry VIII. and grantee of the manor of Orpington as before-mentioned, built a feat in this parifh, in which he magnificently entertained queen Elizabeth, on the 22d of July, 1573; who, on her reception here, was addreffed by a nymph, perfonating the genius of the houfe. Then the fcene fhifted, and from feveral chambers, which, as they were contrived, reprefented a bark, or fhip, and a fea conflict was exhibited to her view; which delighted the queen fo much, that, at her departure, (to perpetuate the memory both of the owner and the entertainment,) fhe gave this houfe the name of *Bark-Hart*,[r] by which it is ftill called, being part of the poffeffions of Sir John Dixon Dyke, bart. of Lullingftone before-mentioned.

CROFTON is a manor, or, as it is now called, *Crawton*, which lies in the midft of the woods, about a mile and a half weftward of Orpington-ftreet. It is faid to have been once a parifh of itfelf, and to have been deftroyed by fire. However that might be, the fcattered foundations of houfes, which the plough frequently turns up, and other fuch remains, fhew it to have been formerly a place of fome fize and confequence.

This place was part of thofe vaft poffeffions, with which William the Conqueror enriched his half-brother Odo, bifhop of Baieux, and it was accordingly entered, under the general title of that prelate's lands, in Domefday as follows:

Anfchitillus holds of the bifhop (of Baieux) Croctune. It was taxed at 1 fuling and 1 yoke. The arable land is .... In demefne there is nothing; but there are 3 villeins and 4 borderers.

In the reign of king Edward I. this place was become the inheritance of Ralph de Wibourn, whofe family was of good efteem and confiderable property in this county, as appears by feveral antient deeds of that time.

[r] Strype's Annals, vol. ii. p. 3139.

time. From this name it went, about the latter end of king Edward III's reign, to Sir Robert Belknap, chief juſtice of the common-pleas, who was attainted and baniſhed into Ireland, in the 11th year of king Richard II. In the 2d year of king Henry IV. this manor eſcheated to the crown, by the death of Juliana his wife,[s] who had been left in poſſeſſion of it by authority of parliament, notwithſtanding her huſband's attainder and baniſhment.[t] In which year, on the petition of Hamon Belknap, their ſon, the parliament enabled him in blood and land to his father, notwithſtanding the judgment made againſt him, as before-mentioned. For though Sir Robert Belknap was permitted by the parliament in the 20th year of that reign, to return from baniſhment, yet his attainder ſtill remained as before. The Belknaps bore for their arms, *Azure, on a bend between two cotizes three eagles diſplayed argent.*

Sir Hamon Belknap left three ſons, John, William, and Henry, each of whom ſucceſſively inherited this manor. The latter, on the death of his two brothers, ſ. p.[u] becoming poſſeſſed of it, reſided at Beccles, in Suſſex. He died in the third year of the reign of king Henry VII. leaving a ſon, Edward, and four daughters. He was ſucceeded in this manor by Edward his ſon, who became a great warrior, and a man of much public action, and was of the privy-council, both to king Henry VII. and VIII. He reſided at Weſton, in Warwickſhire, and was afterwards knighted, and died in the 12th year of that reign, without iſſue; on which his four ſiſters became his coheirs; Elizabeth, married to Sir Philip Cook, of Giddy-hall, in Eſſex; Mary, to George Dannet, of Dannet-hall, eſq. Alice, to Sir William Shelley, and Anne, to Sir Robert Wotton.[w] On a partition of their inheritance, this manor fell to

[s] Rot. Eſch. ejus an. [t] Cott. Records, p. 331.
[u] See Dugd. Warw. p. 408.
[w] Dugd. Warw. p. 409. MSS. pedigree of Butler, of Sudley.

the share of Sir William Shelley, who soon afterwards passed it away by sale to Sir Robert Read, chief justice of the king's bench, in that reign ; who, before the end of it, conveyed it to the hospital of the Savoy in London.

This hospital was suppressed in the 7th year of king Edward VI. a little before his death. Part of the revenue of it, consisting of seven hundred marcs yearly rent in lands, (in which was included this manor of Crofton) was given by the king to the citizens of London, towards maintaining his house of Bridewell, which he had given them at that time, and St. Thomas's hospital, in Southwark. This gift the king confirmed by his charter, on June 26, next following.

On the division of the above-mentioned lands between the two hospitals, this manor was allotted to *St. Thomas's hospital*, part of the possessions of which the inheritance of it still remains, and as such is now vested in the mayor and commonalty of the city of London, Thomas Cope, esq. being the present lessee of it.

There was a *free chapel* at this place, called *Rufferth chantry*, which was suppressed by the act of the 1st year of king Edward VI. and vested in the king : and it appears by the survey then taken,[x] that it was distant two miles from the parish church, that there was a flood between them, by which the people of Crofton were hindered from going thither ; and that there were two chantries more in this chapel.

MAYFIELD PLACE is a seat on the west side of the village of Orpington, being the scite of the small manor of *Little Orpington*, alias *Mayfield*. The latter name of Mayfield, or Mayvil, being its most antient and proper one, which it acquired from a family who formerly held it, as appears by several dateless deeds. Philip de Malevill, or Mayvil, as his name was commonly called, held this manor in the 12th and 13th of

[x] In the Augtn. office.

king John's reign, of Richard de Rokefley, who held it of the archbifhop, as the fourth part of a knight's fee; Malgerius de Rokefle, anceftor of Richard, held it of the archbifhop by knights fervice, in the reign of the Conqueror, as appears by the general furvey of Domefday, in which it is thus entered, under the title of land held of the archbifhop by knights fervice:

Malgerius holds of the archbifhop 3 yokes in Orpington, and it was taxed for fo much without Orpington, in the time of king Edward the Confeffor; now there are 2 yokes within Orpington, and the third without. The arable land is . . . . . . In demefne there is 1 carucate, and 4 villeins, with 1 borderer, and 4 fervants; and half a carucate and 3 acres of meadow, and wood for the pannage of 11 hogs. In the time of king Edward it was worth 40 fhillings, when he received it 20 fhillings, and now 50 fhillings.

When the family of Malevill, or Mayvil, quitted the poffeffion of this manor I do not find; but in the reign of king Edward III. the Rokefleys held it themfelves; for John de Rokefley, grandfon of Gregory, and rector of the church of Chelsfield, in the 33d year of that reign, conveyed it to Sir John Peche, from whom it defcended down to Sir John Peche, knightbanneret, of Lullingftone, who dying without iffue, in the reign of king Henry VIII. Elizabeth his fifter became his heir, and being married to John Hart, efq. of the Middle Temple, he, in her right, became poffeffed of it.[y] His grandfon, Sir George Hart, on the death of his father, in the 22d of queen Elizabeth, had poffeffion granted of the manor of Mayfield, alias Malvyle, and two meffuages, with five hundred acres of land, in Orpington, Chelsfield, Farnborough, and Otford; being held of the king, as of his manor of

[y] Philipott, p. 259. Addenda.

Otford,

Otford, by knights fervice.[z] From him it defcended to his grandfon, William Hart, efq. who died in 1671.

Sir Fifher Tench, bart. of Low Layton, in Eflex, was poffeffed of it in the beginning of the reign of king George I. He had been created a baronet Aug. 8, in the 2d year of that reign ; and bore for his arms, *Argent, on a chevron between three lions heads erafed gules, a crofs croflet or.*[a] He died in 1736, and was fucceeded in the poffeffion of it by his only furviving fon, Sir Nathaniel Tench, bart. who died in 1737, unmarried; on which the title became extinct, and his only furviving fifter, married to Sorefby, became his heir, and he, in her right, became entitled to the manor of Little Orpington, which he foon after fold to Mr. William Quilter, leatherfeller, of London, who new built the manor houfe. He was fheriff of this county in 1747, and died in 1764, having by will devifed it to his niece, Sufannah, who firft married Mr. George Lake of Sevenoke, and next Richard Glode, efq. who on her death became poffeffed of it in his own right. He married fecondly, Martha, daughter of James Olderfhaw, efq. deceafed of Leicefter. He was fheriff of London, and knighted in 1795, and is the prefent owner of this eftate, and at times refides here.

A court baron is held for this manor.

EASTHALL is a manor here, which is fo called from its fituation near the eaftern bounds of this parifh, though great part of the lands belonging to it lie in St. Mary Cray.

In the reign of king Edward I. it was in the poffeffion of the family of Chellesfeld ; one of whom, William de Chellesfeld, in the 13th year of that reign, had a grant of free warren for his lands here, and at other places in this neighbourhood. From this family the manor of Eafthall, with that of Chelsfield, paffed, before the end of that reign, to Otho de Grandifon,

---

[z] Rot. Efch. ejus anni.   [a] Guillim, beft edit. pt. ii. p. 215.

difon, whofe defcendant, Sir Thomas Grandifon, died poffeffed of both in the 50th year of king Edward III. From which time to the 2d year of king Richard III. this manor paffed in the fame tract of ownerfhip as that of Chelsfield did; in which year Ifabel, widow of Henry vifcount Bourchier, and earl of Effex, died poffeffed of them both.

In the next reign of king Henry VII. this manor appears to have been in the poffeffion of Sir Edward Poynings, K. G. fon of Robert, who was a younger fon of Robert lord Poynings. He was a perfon of eminent note, and in great favour with Henry VII. who made him of his privy council, conftable of Dover-caftle, warden of the cinque ports, K. G. &c. By Elizabeth his wife, daughter of Sir John Scott, he had an only fon, who died in his life time, though he left feveral natural children. He died poffeffed of it in the 14th year of king Henry VIII. as was found by the inquifition taken that year. On his death, not only without lawful iffue, but without any collateral kindred, who could make claim to his eftates, this manor, with his other lands, efcheated to the crown,[b] where it continued till king Henry VIII. granted it to Sir Thomas Cromwell, lord Cromwell, afterwards created earl of Effex, on whofe attainder, in the 32d year of that reign, it became again vefted in the crown, and ftaid there till the king, in his 36th year, granted it, among other premifes, to Sir Martin Bowes, to hold *in capite*, by fealty only.[c] He alienated it in the 1ft year of king Edward VI. to Sir Percival Hart of Lullingftone, from whom it defcended lineally to Percival Hart, efq. of Lullingftone, whofe only daughter and heir, Anne, carried it, with many other eftates in thefe parts, to her fecond hufband, Sir Thomas Dyke, bart. of Horeham, in Suffex, and

[b] Philipott, p. 45. [c] Rot. Efch. ejus an. pt. 16.

their only surviving son, Sir John Dixon Dyke, bart. of Lullingstone, is the present possessor of this manor.

It appears by the escheat-rolls of the 28th of king Edward III. that Augustine Wallys then possessed premises called *Bucklers*, in Orpington. King Edward VI. in his 5th year, granted a messuage, formerly DELAHAYS, in Orpington, to Edward lord Clinton and Saye.[d]—The Hon. Richard Spencer, second son of Robert lord Spencer, of Wormleighton, was possessed of a *seat in Orpington*, in which he resided. He died in 1661, leaving by Mary his wife, daughter of Sir Edwin Sandys, bart. of Northborne, two daughters, Mary, married to William Gee, esq. of Bishop's Burton, in Yorkshire; and Margaret, to John Venables, esq. of Cheshire, who became their father's coheirs. William Gee, esq. seems, in right of his wife, to have become possessed of this estate, whose descendant, Richard Gee, esq. afterwards resided here, and died in 1727, having married Philippa, daughter of Sir Nicholas Carew, bart. widow of the Hon. John Beaumont. He was succeeded in it by a son of the same name, who died in 1791, leaving by Elizabeth, daughter and heir of John Holt, esq. two sons, the eldest of whom became intitled to this seat. Before his father's death he took the name and arms of Carew, in pursuance of the will of Sir Nicholas Hacket Carew, bart. who died in 1762; an act having passed for that purpose in 1780, whose estate he likewise at length succeeded to by virtue of the limitations in Sir Nicholas's will. In 1794 he served the office of sheriff of this county, and now resides here. The arms of Gee are, *Gules a sword in bend proper hilted or*.

It appears by the survey, taken in pursuance of the act passed in the 1st year of king Edward VI. for the suppressing of chantries, obits, &c. that there was land in this parish of the clear yearly value of 6s. 8d. which

[d] Augtn. Off. Deeds of Purch. and Excheq. box G. 34.

had

had been given for a sermon, to be preached yearly in the church of Orpington.[e]

There are no *parochial charities*.

ORPINGTON is within the ECCLESIASTICAL JURISDICTION of the *diocese* of Rochester. It is a *peculiar* of the archbishop of Canterbury, and as such is in the *deanry* of Shoreham. The church, which is dedicated to All Saints, is small but neat, and kept in good repair; it consists of one isle, and a chancel at the east end; the screen between them is a curious piece of Gothic work, carved on oak, in good preservation; the spire and part of the tower are shingled; it contains two bells. On the north side of the inner door way, at the west end, is a tomb in the wall, under an arch of stone, of an elliptical or contrasted Gothic form, curiously ornamented; under it is an altar tomb, now boarded over, to form a seat. The entrance, or west door of this church is of Norman construction, as appears by the ornaments about it.

In this church, among others monuments and inscriptions are the following: on a small square board, fixed to the screen on the north side, next to the body of the church, is a memorial for Oliver, third son of Thomas Watts, vicar of this place, and of Aubrey his wife; he died an infant, 1698. *In the great chancel*, on the north side, a memorial for Rd. Gee, esq. ob. 1727; above are these arms quar. 1st and 4th, Gee a sword in bend: 2d and 3d, Spencer; another for Philippa, relict of the above mentioned Richard Gee, obt. 1744. Arms, Gee impaling three lions passant in a lozenge. On a grave stone, a brass plate and inscription in black letter, for William Gulby, esq. obt. 1439; underneath, a shield of arms, a chevron between three cross molines. On a grave-stone, in the middle, before the steps to the altar, is a large brass plate, with the figure of a priest, and inscription in black letter, for Tho. Wilkynson, A. M. preb. of Rippon and rector of Harrow, in Midd. and of Orpington, ob. 1511; on the south side, a mural monument for Mr. Rd. Spencer, 4th son of the Hon. Rd. Spencer, son of Rt. lord Spencer, arms, Spencer, above; below, Spencer, impaling or, a fess dancette between 3 cross croslets fitchee gules. On adjoining grave-stones, within the rails, are memorials for Mary, wife of Wm. Gee, esq. of Bishop's Burton, in

[e] Augm. Off. Survey of Chantries, &c.

Yorkshire,

Yorkshire, one of the daughters and heirs of the Hon. Richard Spencer, ob. 1702; above are the arms of Gee and Spencer quarterly; for Margaret, wife of John Venables, esq. of Agdon, in Cheshire, one of the daughters and heirs of the Hon. Rich. Spencer, ob. 1676; the arms, two bars impaling Spencer. A memorial for the Hon. Mary Spencer, widow of the Hon. Rd. Spencer, daughter of Sir Rich. Sandys of Northborne, obt. 1675, æt. 69; arms, Spencer impaling Sandys. A memorial for the Hon. Rich. Spencer, second son of Robert lord Spencer, baron of Wormleighton, obt. 1661, æt. 68; arms, Spencer with seven quarterings, a crescent for difference. *In the north chancel*, which is a small one, belonging to the seat called Barkhart, in this parish, at the west end, on a grave stone, is a brass plate, with the figure of a priest, and inscription in black letter, for Mr. John Gover, BLL. and vicar of this church, ob. Aug. 6, 1522. On two truss stones of an arch, at the east end, and on the capitals of the columns at the entrance of this chancel, are these arms, 1st, a chevron between three trefoils, 2d as the former, impaling a bend on a chief, two mullets pierced.[f]

In the 15th year of king Edward I. the church of Orpington was valued at sixty marcs, and the vicarage of it at eight marcs.[g]

The church is a sinecure rectory, with a vicarage endowed, to which the church of St. Mary Cray is a chapel, as was formerly the church of Nockholt, which has been many years separated from it, and is now a free parochial chapel, the vicar of Orpington being instituted to this vicarage with the chapel of St. Mary Cray annexed. The vicarage was endowed by Richard archbishop of Canterbury, in 1173, and with a house and a parcel of land by archbishop Courtney, in 1393, which was confirmed by the dean and chapter that same year.[h] In 1687, Robert Say, provost of Oriel college, and rector of this church, on his granting a new lease of this parsonage, bound the lessee to pay annually an augmentation of 26l. 13s. 4d. to the vicar of Orpington cum St. Mary Cray,

[f] See the monum. and inscrip. at large, in Reg. Roff. p. 964.
[g] Stev. Mon. vol. i. p. 456.
[h] Archives of dean and chapter, MSS. A. 11. Regist. Morton, Dene, Bourchier, and Courtney, MSS. Lamb.

which was that year confirmed by the archbifhop and dean and chapter, and entered in the Regifter of the latter.

The rectory is a donative, in the gift of the archbifhop of Canterbury, and is from time to time leafed out by the rector, together with the tithe of wood in Knockholt, the parfonage-houfe, and about fixty acres of glebe land belonging to it. Hugh de Mortimer, rector of this church, releafed the demand of fmall tithes from the priors manor of Orpington.[1]

The rector is patron of the vicarage, and receives 16s. 8d. as a yearly acknowledgement from the vicar, who has 40l. per annum paid him by the leffee of the parfonage. The church of Orpington, with the chapel of St. Mary Cray, is valued in the king's books at 30l. 14s. 4½d. and the yearly tenths at 3l. 1s. 5¼d. The vicarage is a difcharged living of the clear yearly value, as certified, of 45l. the yearly tenths of which are 13s. 9d¾.[k]

By virtue of a *commiffion of enquiry* into the value of church livings, in 1650, iffuing out of chancery, it was returned, that the parfonage of Orpington was a donative, belonging to one Mr. Robinfon, who received forty pounds per annum out of it, and held it by grant from the laft archbifhop of Canterbury, and let it out with the tithe wood in Knockholt, with the parfonage houfe, and forty acres of glebe-land, in Orpington, for certain years, and was worth, *communis annis*, two hundred pounds. That the vicarage belonged to one mafter Joiner, who had forty pounds per annum paid him out of the aforefaid tithes, and that the vicarage, as computed, was worth twenty pounds per annum.[l]

[1] Cart. Antiq. chap. 349, among the archives of the dean and chapter.
[k] Bacon, Lib. Regis.
[l] Parl. Surveys, Lamb. lib. vol. xix.

CHURCH

CHURCH OF ORPINGTON.

PATRONS,
Or by whom presented.

Archbishop of Canterbury............

The Crown, by lapse ....

Rector of Orpington ....

RECTORS.

Hugh de Mortimer, in 1254.[m]
Master Reginald de Brandon, 1293.[n]
Thomas Wilkinson, A. M. obt. Dec. 13, 1511.[o]
Hugh de Mortimer.[p]
John Bancroft, D. D. obt. Feb. 1640.[q]
.... Robinson, 1640.
Robert Saye, in 1687.[r]
Robert Uvedale, LL.D. in 1696.
Henry Hall, A.M. obt. Oct. 31, 1763.[s]
Charles Plumptree, D. D. Nov. 1763, obt. Sept. 14, 1779.[t]
William Backhouse, D. D. Ap. 1780, resigned 1781.
William Clarke, A.M. Mar. 30, 1782.

VICARS.

John Gover, LLB. obt. Aug. 6, 1522.
William Wood, obt. June 1620.[u]
Christopher Monkton, obt. July 1, 1651.[w]
Henry Stiche, obt. Nov. 1670.
Benjamin Blackstone, obt. Jan. 1671.[x]
Robert Bourne, 1671, obt. Nov. 1687.[y]

[m] Chart. Antiq. Cap. Cantuar. He was provost of Oriel college, Oxford.
[n] Prynne's Records, p. 592.
[o] Also rector of Harrow on the Hill, prebendary of Rippon.
[p] Archives of the dean and chapter.
[q] Bishop of Oxford. He lies buried in Cuddesdon church. He held this rectory in commendam. Willis's Cath. vol. ii. p. 433, 553.
[r] Reg. dean and chapter of Canter.

[s] He was also vicar of East Peckham, rector of Harbledown, and treasurer of Wells.
[t] And archdeacon of Ely, and rector of St. Mary Woolnoth, London.
[u] He lies buried in this church.
[w] And rector of Hayes, where he lies buried.
[x] He was buried at Chichester.
[y] He was rector of Hayes, and was buried in this church.

PATRONS, &c.	VICARS.
Rector of Orpington	Thomas Watts, A. M. 1687. resigned 1732.
James Whitehouse, 1732, obt.
Francis Fawkes, A.M. relig. 1755. 1774.[z]
John Till, A. M. 1774.[a]
J. Pratt, 1778. Present vicar.

[z] He resigned this vicarage on being presented to the rectory of Hayes.

[a] He was presented to Hayes in October 1777.

ADDITIONS AND CORRECTIONS

TO THE

FIRST AND SECOND VOLUMES.

ORPINGTON.

PAGE 97. THE VILLAGE of Orpington is situated about a mile from the southern, and half that distance from the northern boundary of it. The Crofton woods are, for the most part, in the parish, and its western boundary runs through them, and in continuation, divides the farm house of Towncourt, which is partly in this parish, and partly in Chesilhurst, and is at present possessed by Mrs. Hodsoll, mother of Miss Matilda Hodsoll. The soil is in general light, some sandy, and some gravelly; but about Crofton it is a cold clay and swampy. The parish contains about sixteen hundred acres. There are two farms of some account here—Patten-grove, belonging to Sir John Dixon Dyke; and Perry-hall, to Sir Richard Glode.

PAGE 112. In the list of the *vicars* of Orpington, correct thus—

James Whitehouse, inducted 1732, obt. 1755.
Francis Fawkes, A. M. inducted 1755, resigned 1794.
John Till, A. M. inducted 1774, resigned 1778.
J. Pratt, inducted 1778. Present vicar.